INDEX

1.INTRO

It is the year 2021, Joe Biden just became the next American President. But all is not well. We have seen the storming of the Capitol, riots were everywhere and the year is only beginning.

But let´s not forget 2020, the worst year in a long time.

Not only did we have an increased amount of natural disasters, there was the whole "Black lives matter" movement, which in it´s core is a good thing but it came with a lot of demonstrations, riots etc....

Alongside you had the still ongoing "climate change" movement with basically the same results, demonstrations, riots...

But nothing kept us more on the tip of our toes like the Corona virus, also named COVID-19.

And while at first people were relaxed about it, it won´t be that bad, it will pass just like the flue, it doesn´t do that much damage, as soon as governments started to take actions, the first conspiracy theories popped up.

It was all a global plan and suddenly, everywhere you heard the same words repeated: Big pharma, Big industry, Big oil, the Big reset....

Governments were trying to make us in to slaves without a quality living, they wanted to downsize the population and we were just puppets in their evil game.

And let´s not forget, according to some, Bill Gates was the evil master mind behind all of this. Because first he had gotten us all hooked on computers and everything that comes with it and now, working together with governments from around the world, he would make sure that everyone has to take a vaccine with a nano chip in it.

Like this, the "New World Order" would come in to effect, dominating a world that where we would be nothing more than cheap labor forces and where only the richest people would have a nice life.

Now let´s make one thing very clear. NO, this virus was not an evil masterplan.

In fact, most industries suffered a lot over the year 2020, so Big industry for sure wasn´t too thrilled about 2020.

Big pharma then? No, not really. Although they had to come up with the vaccine, it neither was a year for them where they suddenly began to make leaps in profits. Simply because, yes they are going to make serious money from the vaccines, all the rest was put on hold and to top it all off, people were getting less sick just because they weren´t going out that much, they weren´t getting hurt that much for the same reason etc....

Aaaah but the richest people were only getting richer in 2020, while we the working people were suffering.

Elon Musk became the new richest man on the planet.

And of course we also had Jeff Bezos, whom made huge profits with Amazon.

Surely, this was all part of the master plan of the "NWO"?

Well no. Musk is getting to see more and more profit of the several he has been running already for some years now. Tesla numbers are getting better and better, Space X is finally good and well running and so on, and so on.

And Bezos? Well actually, isn´t it a bit

normal that in a world where a lot of places are closed, where people have to order more and more online, that he wouldn´t make more profit?

Both men were doing just fine and for sure didn´t need a virus to make more profit.

No, forget the "New World Order" idea, it just doesn´t make any sense.

But that doesn´t mean there isn´t a "World Order". That has existed practically since Columbus discovered the new world and has been in place ever since.

In this book i will show you how the world is run, not by governments, but by a few elite. Sometimes the seats at the table are filled in differently, times change and needs change, but the "World Order" always stays in place.

And while we still think we live in a democracy, at least the most of us, this is just an illusion. Even the biggest democracy on earth, the good old U.S.A., is far from being one.

2.PRE-COLOMBIAN

If the idea of one force, one group or even one person having total control over a civilization sounds weird to you, think again. It is in fact, a tale as old as time.

As soon as the first civilizations start to appear, you always see one dominating force.

For sure, it wasn´t world dominating but it did was a domination over a large area and most of the times it was one person who had the absolute power.

In the East we had the Chinese empire, which, at his height, was the biggest empire ever seen.

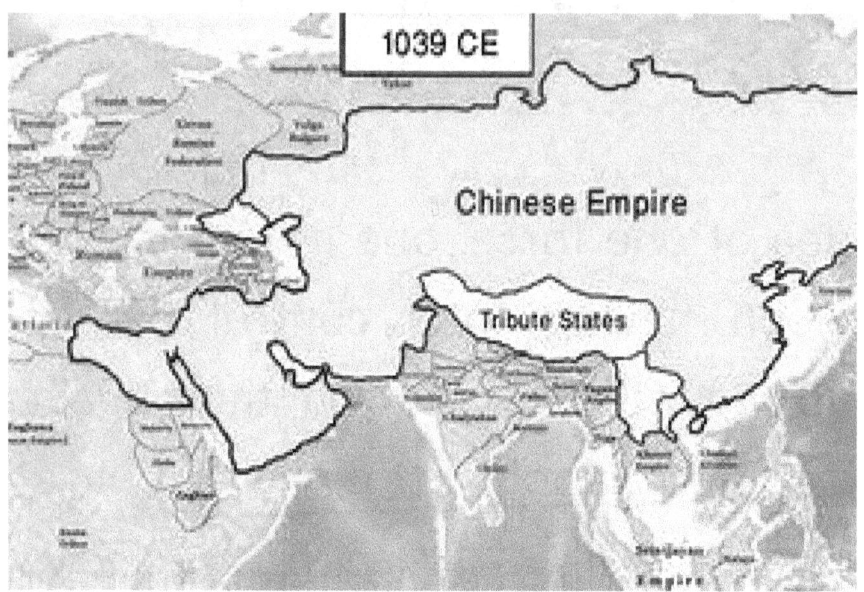

And it was ruled by one man.

But of course you also had the Roman empire and in the Americas the Incan empire and Mayan, Aztec etc....

All these empires had one thing in common, they were all ruled by one person.

This person was the personification of god or the gods and his word was law.

It is true that these emperors always had

advisors at their side. Sometimes that came in the form of wise men, other times senators, but more often than not priests, witches, etc...

But at the end of the it was, it was the emperor who made the decision and so influencing and controlling millions of people.

But that didn´t mean they were untouchable. A lot of times, these rulers came to an unwanted death. Or they were killed by the people around them who wanted all the power to themselves, or they were simply killed by the people if they went too far in their rules and demands.

A famous example of this is Moctezuma, emperor of the Aztecs.

Although he had a divine status, when the Spaniards arrived, he made so many bad decisions that, eventually, the people turned against him and killed him. But by that time, it was too late and the Aztec empire would come to an end.

This is only one example but you see this all

over the world that sooner or later all these regimes with absolute power would come to an end, one way or the other.

But we still had a long way to go.

3. THE TRUE START OF THE WORLD ORDER

With the discovery of the Americas in 1492, Spain became the first real world order.

It was Columbus who in 1492, sponsored by the Spanish crown, set off towards the west, sure that he would find a faster way to sail to Asia and India.

Up till then there were 2 possibilities for going over there. One was by land, which was actually faster than over sea, but that also meant that not as much trade could come back to Europe, and the other was by sea. Sailing to the Indies and Asia was not for the faint hearted. Especially around the southern tip of Africa ships would, more often than not, experience heavy seas and storms. But it did mean you could come back with a much bigger cargo.

Although the fact that the knowledge of the earth being a globe had been around for thousands of years, in the middle ages not a lot of people were convinced of that, more so, the theory of the earth being flat was more accepted than ever.

But that was not counting Columbus.

The man was absolutely convinced that there was a faster trade route by sailing to the west. Convincing someone to sponsor an expedition would proof to be something else.

He tried to find money in Italy and Portugal but was rejected as soon as he started talking about the world not being flat. But then, he went to the Spanish court.

Spain at that time was a newly united Spain and their monarchs were Ferdinand and Isabella.

Although they were not convinced either about the world being a globe, they did see an opportunity. If they would sponsor this voyage and Columbus would indeed find a faster trade route, this would mean that this new united Spain would become a dominant force in Europe because, if this would be true, and they could control this route, it would bring more wealth to Spain than any other country. And who knows, if any lands would be discovered, they could be conquered and like that expand the territory of the Spanish crown.

What happened next, everybody knows of course. The Americas were discovered and Spain became richer and more powerful than ever before and would continue to be a dominating world power until the 19th century.

In fact, with all the riches soon coming in Spain became so powerful, it expanded the army and soon were not satisfied with just having enormous territories overseas, also central Europe had to suffer the might of the Spanish crown. Further more, there was the alliance with the Holy church. Spain was already very religious, some even said that Ferdinand and Isabella were more religious than the Pope, and this alliance made sure they could spread their power even faster over Europe.

It didn´t even took a century before Spain was master of the world.

(Spanish empire by 1582)

And what about the rest of the mayor players at that time i hear you say.

Well it did take some time before the rest could catch up.

The taste for power of the Spaniards was so great that other big countries like France, Germany and England had all the trouble in the world just to keep the Spaniards out, that for a long while it didn´t even enter in their heads to start exploring for themselves.

It would take until the beginning of the 17th century before that would change.

England had been busy fighting off the Spaniards in the 16th century under Queen Elisabeth.

And although Elisabeth was successful in doing so, she was so concerned about any new attempts by the Spaniards, that any requests of setting up expeditions to the new world fell upon deaf ears.

It was her successor James I that would change that.

Almost as soon as he became King he set up expeditions to the new world which would result in the first colony already being founded in 1607. It would be Virginia that would have the honor of being the first American colony of England, followed by Massachusetts in 1620 and New Hampshire in 1623.

And just like with Spain, it didn´t take long for England to become the other mayor player in world dominance. In fact, their colonies grew more or less as fast than the Spanish, which by 1732 would result in the famous 13 colonies on American land.

THE ORIGINAL 13 COLONIES

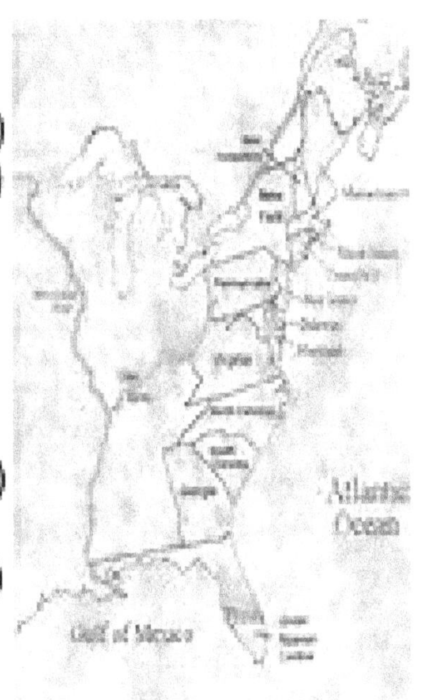

And all seemed well. Spain and England were ruling the world and were smart enough, some minor conflicts aside, not to make each others life difficult.

But that was until 1775, when the thirteen colonies of England decided they had enough and rebelled. It would be the start of a whole new dynamic and a change also of whom would be the true world leaders.

4.USA: BOUGHT AND PAID FOR

When is say, bought and paid for, of course i don´t mean that literally but yes, in a sense it was like that.

Everybody who knows a bit of American history of course knows the story of the revolution. How the people had enough of being considered just a colony where the British could do as they pleased while the Americans did not even have representation in the British government. And yes, so far so good, yes basically this was the reason why the revolution started, but did they really wanted separation from the motherland? Did Great Britain really want to keep on to USA? Was Great Britain really the winner of this revolution? Let´s take a closer look.

So let´s start from the beginning. As i said already, people already were not happy with the way things were going but that all came to a climax with the famous "Boston tea party". This was a protest organized by the "Sons of Liberty" in Boston, Massachusetts, on December 16, 1773.

It was a reaction to the Tea act of May 10 0f that same year, which allowed the British West India Company to sell tea from China and the Indies without paying taxes, apart from those imposed by the Townshend

Acts. American patriots had enough of their rights being violated and that resulted in an entire shipment of tea being destroyed as a way of protest.

The British government of course could not let this just pass by and had to react, which in turn led to the American revolution.

So, so far so good and everybody knows

what happened next. but do they?

Let's have a look at the logistics first.

If you take a closer look at both sides, you will see that the amount of men fighting might be considered more or less the same.

The British army officially had 48,647 soldiers at the time of the revolution.

39,294 infantry

6,869 cavalry

2,484 artillery.

Estimations are that this number went up a whole lot if you take the militia in account, in total it could have been as much as 500,000 men fighting for the British.

From American side however, they weren´t with much less. Although there was not an official army yet for the US, every colony did provide soldiers.

The official numbers talk about between 80,000 and 100,000 soldiers. And with militia they would have been around 400,000.

From both sides there were other countries involved, as we well know. The British for the most part had German support, while the patriots could count on the support of French and Spanish allies.

But here is where we have to start and have a look at reality.

Under the reign of King George III, the British army was the best trained and disciplined army in the world.

Some of the arguments like that terrain knowledge was a disadvantage for the British just don´t hold up. They had more than enough support from the loyalists who knew the terrain as well as the patriots.

Furthermore they had a much greater firepower than the patriots.

So how was it possible that the British army was defeated?

Let´s have look at the global picture. Great Britain was the dominating power in the world, together with the Spanish, although the power of the Spanish was already in a downward spiral.

For Great Britain there were colonies of much greater importance than the 13 colonies. China, the West Indies and the Caribbean just to name some. These were much more important, simply because they brought much more money than the US.

In the US, the cotton industry was still a

very small industry. The oil industry hadn´t started yet, as the gold rush.

The biggest industry at time for the British was sugar, making for example the Caribbean much more valuable than the US, purely seen from an economic viewpoint.

It is no big surprise then that, once the British army came upon much more resistance than they could have predicted, there were already very soon voices in Britain to just cut the colonies loose and focus on the more important ones.

It was actually only because of King George being stubborn and not willing to give up, along with some of his generals, that the war kept on going.

And it would keep going until 1783, when a final to this conflict was already far past due.

Not only did Great Britain have other troubles than to fight colonies in the US, the public opinion back in Great Britain wan turning more and more against King George.

The Caribbean for example were under siege. While the British initially focused on the US, the French and Spanish took advantage of that to try to take control over the Caribbean, knowing that would mean a boom for their economy.

And the British government wasn´t having it anymore.

So peace talks were started once the Caribbean was recovered.

And it has to be said, not even after these talks and the independence of the US, the British really came out as the losing party, you might even say they were the winner.

In the peace declaration it was stated that Great Britain would keep Canada, also the British could keep some of their military forts in the US to protect their trade with the Native Americans. Combine this with the fact that the US was becoming a burden, that there was no more need to send troops and equipment over, coupled with the fact that a lot of Americans still depended on the export From Britain, i think you are beginning to get the picture of who really was the victor in this conflict.

Yes, USA became an independent nation, but at what cost?

But it doesn´t stop there. We all know July 4 as the signing of the declaration of independence, but not even that was true.

The declaration was officially signed by all persons involved on August 2. Official sources will tell you that this was because several people couldn´t agree on the content but there are other sources that state this was not the only problem. Many also had questions about signing members.

Take the case of Henry Laurens.

He was a merchant, rice planter and slave trader. For a short while he even was

President of congress and was seen as one of the true leaders of the revolution. But that all would change after he was captured by the British while on a trade mission to the Netherlands. He was send to the Tower of London, only to be released in 1781 in exchange for Lord Cornwallis.

Many speculate that it was during this time in prison that he became a loyalist again. The fact that once back in the US he didn´t do nothing anymore to further the case of the patriots, only fueled that suspicion. Also, after the independence he withdrew from public life although he had several offers to stay in politics.

But he wasn´t the only one. Even one of the most famous founding fathers, Benjamin Franklin, wasn´t free of suspicion.

Not only were there some questioning how loyal Franklin was to the cause. The time that he spend in Europe did not only make sure of the alliance with France, but he also was very popular in Great Britain, which was enough for some to begin to whisper that Franklin really wasn´t that much of a patriot.

Another factor was his son William.

He was the acknowledged illegitimate son of Benjamin. Not only was he a convinced loyalist throughout the revolution, he was also the last colonial Governor of New Jersey. And that of course didn´t help the case of Benjamin because, as some stated, if he can not even convince his own son, is that because the son is so convinced or because the father is not totally convinced of the cause and he only supports the revolution for personal gain?

In any case, it is estimated that right after the revolution there was still a staggering amount of loyalist, some sources talk about between 300,000 and 400,000.

Many of them very influential and rich people who, although they agreed with the independence, only saw this as a stepping stone to gather even more power and wealth in this new nation with few rules. Some becoming so powerful that they would have a hand in electing the Presidents of the USA.

And in the future, people like that would become part of the world power, although they themselves not in politics or royalty, mighty enough to have, not only a say, but sometimes a decisive factor in world events.

5. THE INDUSTRIAL REVOLUTION

USA for a large part stayed a minor player on the world stage. It was more a place for fortune seekers or simply people wanting a new start a in life.

Of course there was the goldrush in this ever expanding country, the cotton industry was booming, even the weapon industry was really taking off, but all of that did not really make an impact on the world stage.

But that was soon about to change with the industrial revolution. Not only was there once again the British influence but also thanks to some very brilliant men whom were about to change the world and how that world was ruled. No longer a monopoly of monarchs and governments but by hard cash.

The industrial revolution started somewhere around the turn of the century in the beginning of the 1800s.

This sounded in the start of the switch from pure manual labour to machine production. In the beginning this was with water and steampower but would soon change thanks to the oil industry.

This machine powered production led to new ways of producing iron but what was really the industry that benefitted the most in the beginning was the textiles industry.

Great Britain was again the main player in this revolution and soon they spread their technology not only over their empire but also invested in countries in mainland Europe.

Factories of textiles, iron and coal were first introduced by the British in Belgium. Both countries were linked by the monarchy, King Leopold I of Belgium was not only family, he also was smart enough to have interest in these new technologies and convinced the British to invest in his newly founded country.

But of course the industrial revolution also went to the US.

For a little while we see that, although huge leaps were made, we were at a status quo again. Big cities were getting even bigger thanks to the industry, some people even richer, but that was about it. But then came what historians call, the second industrial revolution.

The oil industry put it´s foot in the door and it would become a major player, if not the most important.

The oil industry was really started by Edwin Drake in 1859.

While petroleum oil was known before this, there wasn´t really a market for it.

Drake was the first one to put an effective drilling process in place. It was thanks to his methods that the oil industry really could take off.

By the 1870s, this new industry would help a new industrial revolution all over the world but especially in the US, where, as i mentioned in the previous chapter, still were a lot of people with interests in both USA and Great Britain.

A prime example of this was Andrew Carnegie.

Carnegie was born in Scotland and stayed there until he was 12 and his parents decided to emigrate.

As an adult he would be a railroad man first but he quickly realized that the railroad industry was already pretty much a monopoly of Cornelius Vanderbilt.

Vanderbilt, at that time one of the richest people in the world, had made his money first in shipping but saw that with a nation quickly expanding that there would be a bigger demand for railroads than for ships.

So Carnegie decided he would seek his fortune in other areas.

He became a bonds salesman, seeking people in Europe that would and could invest in the American industry, he invested in the new oil industry but yet again, he quickly saw that also there was one man that was already lightyears ahead of him, namely John D. Rockefeller.

But that didn´t mean he had no more paths to choose.

Carnegie saw an opportunity in the steel industry. When the iron industry in Europe jumped over to steel, steel being better quality and more durable, Carnegie already knew about this new process long before any potential competitors in the US. And so steel it would be. He took some huge risks, not only by investing in this new way of manufacturing but also by bidding on a new project in St. Louis.

St. Louis needed a bridge over the Mississippi river, basically connecting the Eastern with the Western frontier and Carnegie did not only outbid his competitors, he also vowed that he would do it faster than anyone else and that his bridge would be stronger than any other bridge including iron.

He won the bid, but convincing the people was something else.

Already while building the bridge Carnegie heard about the rumours that the people didn´t trust this new process, many even saying that they would never cross the bridge out of fear that the steel, once with enough people and transport on it, simply wouldn´t hold the weight.

So Carnegie knew that he would have to do something special once the bridge was finished, to earn the trust of the people in this new product.

The answer was that with the opening of the bridge, he would have an elephant to cross the bridge first.

Not so much for the weight of the elephant but it was a popular belief that they had a sixth sense that prevented them to set foot on an unsafe structure.

The stunt worked and the Carnegie name was set. Carnegie steel would grow out the be one the biggest steel manufacturers in the world, if not the biggest.

When in 1901 he decided to sell Carnegie steel to J.P. Morgan, he was already one of the richest people on the planet but he would officially become the richest, at least for a while.

Carnegie was one of the original tycoons of industry but it wouldn´t stop there.

Together with others just like him, he quickly realized that, when you have enough money to spend, you can just about do anything you want to and get away with it. A little bit later i will tell you all about that but first let me introduce you to the other mayor players of the industrial revolution.

I already mentioned two of them so i will start them first.

First of all, J.P. Morgan.

Morgan was not only a banker but also a very smart business man. He already was the son of a banker but also, again, we see the British connection here. Although he was born in the USA, he spend his early life in Great Britain where he also made his first career steps, following the example of his father, whom he would soon outgrow.

Only a year after he started working for his

father, he moved back to the USA to start working in the New York branch of the company of his father and his meteoric rise would start.

Through several very smart business deals, some might even say almost criminal deals, he only got richer and richer. For example, during the Civil war, he bought up large quantities of outdated rifles for only 3,50 Dollars each, only later arranged it to resell them at 22 Dollars, a lot of them even back to the army, who only found out their error later, but by then it was much too late.

Morgan himself actually never served in the Civil war, just because he paid off officials.

But that would color the life of Morgan throughout his whole life, making profit where possible, ethical or not.

He specialized in buying troubled

companies, only to set up a new structure thanks to his many connections and make big profits.

But besides the deal with Carnegie of which i talked earlier, probably his biggest coup, was after the economic depression of 1893 and would make more powerful than the President of the USA.

The Federal Treasury was almost out of gold in its reserves and President Grover Cleveland went to Morgan for help.

(Grover Cleveland)

They soon reached an agreement to create a private union on Wall Street to provide the Treasury with 65 million Dollars worth in gold, half of that coming from, yes you guessed it, Europe. It saved the Treasury but there was outrage amongst the people and also in Cleveland´s own party. the Democratic party. And it didn´t stop there because Morgan, along with others, with even go further. But more about that later, first let me introduce you to another important part, if not the most important, John D. Rockefeller.

I think most of us know the story of Rockefeller, so i will make it short.

He was of course the founder of Standard oil. But although at one point the government decided that enough was enough with the monopoly of Standard oil, they actually did very little about it. They forced Rockefeller to split up his company into several smaller ones, but that did very little to his power and control over the oil industry.

In fact, the Rockefeller family would continue to dominate oil industry until after WWII, when the Arab countries would make a meteoric rise to power.

But don´t get me wrong, the list of companies that came from the split up of Standard oil, still to this day are main players. I think everybody knows companies as Exxon and Chevron.

So it´s not hard to imagine that Rockefeller, by the time of his death in 1937, is said to have been the richest man there has ever lived. His fortune at that time would have been, in today´s money, at around 300 billion Dollars.

But he, along with Carnegie and Morgan and other players, would do something that, although it would become public knowledge later, would set the tone about who really were the powerhouses in the world and would show to the people that the world is not led by royals and politicians alone, but that there was a new elite, and it would be an elite that not only would be satisfied with total power in their own country but went after world power.

The threesome, along with other players from the weapons industry and the banking world, decided they had enough of playing under government rules. So they decided to buy the Presidency and they succeeded.

They found the right person for the job in the Republican party. The name was William McKinley.

McKinley was a willing victim. He was very ambitious but he also knew that in normal circumstances he couldn´t win the elections. So he gladly accepted the offer that came from this group of very wealthy men. Not only they set up a very large election campaign(something that only grew larger with time), but employees of the companies owned by the group were made very clear that if they didn´t vote for McKinley, life could get very difficult.

McKinley would serve two terms, making new laws whom encouraged commercial activity of course and the tone was set for what would happen from now on, a few men that would decide the fate of not only the USA, but also of the world.

Because, yes, it all came out in public, but the basic idea of what happened attracted even more powerful players.

The Rothschilds for example. This rich banking family originating in Germany, already had a financial empire at that time but they liked the idea of what had happened in the USA.

Of course they already had very strong ties with both monarchies and the political world in Europe and outside that, but actually owning them never came in to play up till that moment.

But soon, all of them joined forces because, if this could be done in the USA, why not expand it across the world?

And so this world order was formed, not so publicly this time, even in secret and it would consist of all these very rich people and the most important Royal ones, the British crown of course being the most important of Royalty.

From now on, the world would never be the same and although the general public still would be in the notion that they live in true democracies, the truth is, true democracy was dead and buried from now on.

6.THE 20th CENTURY

And just like that, we are in the 20th century.

A century that would define the word "world power". USA was becoming the true powerhouse in the world and big cash was king. As we have already seen, even the office of President could be bought(and according to some still is) and this new elite of extremely rich men would also start to dictate what happened, helped with some of the most powerful Royal houses in Europe.

All the USA needed was that little push to really establish itself as the leader of the free world and it wouldn´t have to wait very long. In 1914 the first World War would start and although USA only entered very late in the game, it would define the power balance in the world.

Once the war was finished, it was very clear, the allies had won but more important, USA came out as the great victor.

Great Britain already had stretched its power in mainland Europe by means of industry, but now there was a vacuum. The German Reich had crashed and many business men, backed with American money and even Americas themselves saw their chance of gaining more power in this new power vacuum.

Even our favorite and beloved soft drink Coca Cola were quick to see the opportunity that this new Europe gave, establishing themselves in Germany in 1929. The myth that it was soldiers of the second World War that introduced Europe to Coca Cola can be burried once and for all.

In fact, it is one of those other popular brands of Coca Cola, Fanta, that was invented in Germany.

Because Hitler and the Nazi party were against almost anything American, the head of the German Coca Cola plant, Max Keith had to device a new strategy.

Although Coca Cola was never officially forbidden, the sales went down very quickly once the Nazis were in power and so, after some brainstorming, Fanta was born and still today is one of the principal brands of the Coca Cola company.

This of course being a simple example of how, in a short period of time, the world was changing.

But this of course is a bit of a side track of what was really going on.

Thanks to the first World War, American

industry found it´s way to Europe. The ever expanding industrial industry needed oil, and where do you think that oil was coming from? Further more, thanks to that same war, the weapons industry made huge leaps. Not only did they had to provide millions of weapons during that war, millions more were sold just to maintain that peace. And so the weapons industry got a seat at the table of World Power.

But let´s not get ahead of our selfs.

Back in the States in the beginning of the 20th century, there were other things that would shape the world.

First of all there was prohibition that started after WW1. In 1920 the government decided that there would be a total ban on selling, producing and consuming alcoholic products.

Foreign Vessels
Now Carry Our
Tourist Trade
ALL GETTING
AMERICAN DOLLARS

PROHIBITION
Is Ruining Our
Merchant Marine
600 American Ships
LAID UP TO BE DOCKS

4,000,000
AMERICAN SOLDIER
FOUGHT FOR LIBERTY
AND WERE REWARDED
WITH PROHIBITION
HOW COME ?

TO CONGRESS!
YOU CARE FOR OUR
CRIPPLED SOLDIERS,
OUR MEDALS WILL
CURE 100 THOUSANDS!

WE
WANT
BEER

WE
WANT
BEER

WE
WANT
BEER

WE
WANT
BEER

And just let´s say this wasn´t the smartest move the government ever did. It not only caused huge unrest with the population but it would be responsible for the rise of the maffia, the weapons industry would make huge profits and politicians would become more corrupt than ever.

But like i said, the maffia was the organization that would profit the most.

Where before prohibition they were more focused on local control over an area, they now went global. Through the sale of illegal alcohol, that they bought in Europe or in illegal breweries and distilleries, they would soon become so powerful that it didn´t take all that long before the world power decided to give them a seat at the table.

The prohibition ended by 1933 but by then the harm was done. The people behind the scenes, who truly control the world, had become even more powerful.

So what about the great depression? Someone for sure is asking that question but to be honest, while the majority of the people all over the world were suffering, our powerplayers didn´t suffer a lot of losses, in fact, in some cases they made a lot of money. Just to give an example, real estate became so cheap that the big players took advantage of that, making them only richer.

But there was yet another player entering the scene in the beginning of the 20th century, the pharmaceutical industry.

Although doctors, hospital already had become well established, they were very limited in what they could do. They could fix a broken leg or arm most of the times, if not amputation was often the solution. But that wasn´t safe neither. Often the wound would get infected and there was little to cure it.

They could stitch you up also if you had an open wound but that was about it.

It is isn´t remarkable that many people refused to see a doctor or go to a hospital, because the chances that you would be getting better, weren´t all that high.

Real medicines weren´t that much around. There were many epidemics such as cholera, malaria, plague, typhoid and polio.

But scientists were doing research and the goal was very simple, to develop and make medicines that would benefit the masses.

And those changes were going to come.

The beginning of the 20th century marked the discovery of many new chemical entities that turned out to be remarkable drugs.

And then, finally, in 1928, there was the discovery of penicillin by Dr. Alexander Fleming.

It was the gateway to the discovery and commercialization of more antibiotics and anti-bacterial drugs and labs would start to pop up everywhere, and pharma would become big pharma.

Because, as always, where there is money to be made, there are two sides.

Labs would go with their drugs to doctors and hospitals and especially at the start would offer them a percentage or other kind of rewards if the doctors would make sure that patients would use a specific drug.

So doctors and hospitals profited and the labs profited even more. Pretty soon, especially after WWII, the pharmaceutical industry would boom and become a billion dollar industry. Need i say that they became the next seat at the table of the powers that control the world?

And if that wasn´t enough, yet another player would get a seat at this table, the Arabian oil industry.

The first official discovery of oil in Saudi Arabia was in 1938, by Americans, in Dammam, modern day Dhahran.

Although there had been prior discoveries, they were never exploited for commercial gain and there was a very good reason for that.

First of all, Saudi Arabia itself only became a kingdom in 1932. Second, it had always been difficult to explore for oil due to the instability in the region and third, the first World War and the Great depression also had a part to play in it.

But let´s go back a little bit.

In 1925 Major Frank Holmes signed a concession with the Sheikh of Bahrain, allowing him to search for oil.

Of course, to do so you need money and where better to find money for such an enterprise than in the oil industry itself.

And it was in the States that he would find

that funding, namely with Gulf Oil in 1927.

But Gulf Oil was forced to transfer its interests however, to Standard Oil of California, due to previous agreements with other companies. (and we all know who owned SOC).

It was this company who finally struck oil and at the same time changing the Middle East forever.

Although the Rockefellers couldn´t believe their luck, the deal wouldn´t las forever.

The government soon realized what wealth this new discovery gave and so decided to, slowly but surely, take a bigger piece of the profits by increasing taxes, changing agreements etc....

This is what actually caused the oil crisis in the 70s because both parties were drifted so far apart by now, the bomb was about to explode.

Finally, by 1988, ARAMCO(the new company that was founded by Standard Oil) was officially bought out by Saudi Arabia.

This was the start of never seen riches for the Arabs, seeing that they were sitting on the biggest oil reserve in the world. And yes, they soon became part of the elite group of the World order.

Of course we all know there had been already attempts by the Americans to take the control back over the Arabian oil industry, or at least a part of it, through warfare.

And this is one of those prime examples where you can see that it´s not the politicians that rule the world but other forces. The best example of course being

Iraq where American troops invaded the country, so called because they were producing weapons of mass destruction, but we found out pretty fast that this was not the case, and that the real goal was the recovery of oil fields.

Because don´t get me wrong, yes the mighty of this world do have some agreement and where ever they can work together, they will, but if they see an opportunity to stab each other in the back, they will take it.

So by the end of the 20th century the cards were pretty much shuffled. The big industries ruled the world, sometimes you would have some other industries, like the tobacco industry, who would come knocking at the door, but really, their influence was not nearly enough to have a permanent seat at the high table.

And don´t get me wrong, yes there are of course billionairs that, on their own made a lot of money, putting them on the top spot of richest man in the world but real power is about so much more than that.

The ground works were established in the beginning of the 20th century and the power remains in a very select group of people. There is no use of starting to search for exact numbers in wealth, just because these people have split up their investments in so many ways, there is just no way of keeping track. Let´s just say that the richest man in the world at any given time now might be the richest individual, he or she wouldn´t even come close to the combined wealth of some families or groups.

But more about that in the next chapter where things go wild.

7.MODERN TIMES

Just like in the movie by Charlie Chaplin, that painted a not too positive picture of those times, these "modern times" are also not exactly what you might call a representation of a perfect human civilization.

And it all started already before the year 2000 even started.

Doomsday prophets all over the world were warning us, the end was coming, the year 2000 would be the end of us.

Computers all over the world would stop working, dumping us in to chaos, the anti-Christ was going to come etc....you can not imagine it or was certain, this would be the end of the world.

But of course, like always in these cases, nothing happened.

The next scare would be the 12-21-12.

An ancient Mayan calendar was running at its end and again, this would be the end and yet again, we survived, lucky us.

But all joking aside, what began to worry a lot of people was the ever growing way that being politically correct was thrusted upon us.

Let´s get one straight, i am in every way against racism, prejudice etc... and all for equality but should it be forced upon us, isn´t it very human to know the difference between right and wrong? I strongly believe morality was always inside of us even before any religion, so why in these modern times were some people so desperately searching for justice, to not be offended, to be included in everything ....????

And where did all this come from? Why did we become a "shame culture"?

Well first of all there were the politicians. Suddenly they wanted to play good mothers and fathers for the population, never mind that the population wasn´t asking for that or wanted that, no no, we will decide for you what is correct and how you need to live.

A famous example of this is the smoking ban. I guess everyone with a little bit of a brain knows that smoking is bad for you. But did we really need the politicians to tell us that? Of course not.

Before all these smoking bans just about anywhere, there was already very large percentage of people quitting smoking and many young people didn´t even wanted to start with it. And that is a good thing. So why were these smoking bans even necessary or who did they benefit?

Well actually it benefitted no one. Bars and restaurants saw their income decline because nobody wanted to stay as much time as before if they were a smoker. And standing outside in the street, getting a quick smoke or sitting in a smoking room, where allowed, just doesn´t have the same appeal.

But look at it the other way, for sure the tobacco industry took some real damage? Well no, in fact, they made more profit, so in a way you could say that they were the only ones that had any benefit from these smoking bans. And why? Well it's pretty obvious. Because they didn't have to spend large amounts on advertising, they were only gaining more.

But like i said, this was one of the most famous examples. More and more laws came into effect where you really had the question, what will this do anyone any good?

And in the last years it really has gotten absurd, warnings everywhere, don't do this or if you do this it might cause you harm etc...Yes thank you but i think i know where to draw a line. I know that if i eat a family sized bag of chips, it won´t be the most healthy choice, no need to point that out on the package.

But of course it isn´t just politicians whom made these new modern times rather strange and unsettling. There is an even greater monster that caused a lot more damage and it´s called the internet.

There are two main players we have to thank for the revolution in the computer world, Steve Jobs and Bill Gates.

Now of course, i know, they didn´t do it alone, but let´s just call them our main characters.

And no, they weren´t the first to produce computers or systems but they did start a revolution.

With both their companies(Apple and Microsoft) their goals were very simple, to bring computers to the masses and like that create a better life, both private as work. And so they did. In the 90s of the previous century they made it so that it became very normal to have a computer in your home. And it was only the start of something much bigger.

In that same decade the internet took off. Initially a place where everybody in the world could be connected, with freedom of speech and mind, a place where everybody could do something. But it wouldn´t stat like that for very long time.

Websites shot out of the ground like it was nothing and pretty soon there was something to find for everybody´s liking, making instant millionaires of some creators of websites because of the simple reason that, when a site becomes very popular, automatically you will have companies that want to advertise.

But the first real notion we got of censorship was when the music sharing sites started to pop up.

At first seen as a positive way to simply share music, the music world soon found out there was a more negative to all of this, namely, they weren´t selling any records anymore. It was enough for one individual to buy an album or song, download it to a sharing it, and it could be copied over and over.

It wasn´t a big surprise that soon the music industry started to complain about this and one lawsuit followed the next one. And they got what they wanted, the music sharing websites were forced to shut down. But where the music industry probably thought that it was back to business as usual, they couldn´t have been more wrong.

The musical landscape was changed for ever. Their music was copied so many times by now, people just found other ways to share the music digitally.

But it did brought one positive thing, performers soon realized that they had to convert back to the old ways and perform more often, which in turn was good for the fans.

But the musicians also found other outlets, thanks to websites like youtube they soon found out they could earn money by putting their music on platforms like that.

And where were Jobs and Gates meanwhile? They had become among the richest people in the world.

But did they get a seat at the world table? No not really. Although they had a lot of influence it was rather the other way around. The real World order used their medium to consolidate their power. The world had become a village and soon it would take a very wrong turn.

In 2004 a new website would see the light of day, named Facebook and it would change the world and how interact forever.

Enter Mark Zuckerberg. The creator(although some claim he didn´t but that is another topic) of Facebook actually a very simple idea. Create a platform where people can connect with each other, see what the other one is up, post what you are doing and even search for like minded people or just follow people who you find interesting.

It seemed innocent enough, a sort of digital meeting place, what could go wrong?

Well what could go wrong was, it became too big. It became a world wide phenomenon and soon almost everyone was on Facebook. But with that also came the problem that major news sources also began to publish, from sports to politics, from art to science and everything you can think of in between.

And that was the real problem. Where in the past you would read the news and maybe post your opinion about it, in order to show it to the people you are connected with and share your point of view, the news media made it so that everybody from around the globe could enter their opinion in an open platform, who would have guessed it would lead to extremes? (Enter a laugh whenever you want)

And here is where it all starts to explode.

Suddenly it seemed that in a lot of cases, a normal discussion about a topic wasn´t possible anymore. People felt safe from behind their computer, smartphone .... and thought they could say whatever they wanted. So Facebook decided to step in.

Suddenly there was not only Facebook themselves who began controlling posts, users also could report people who they found offensive.

Now i am not saying   that being politically correct was invented by Facebook but it sure did anything possible make sure that everything was as neutral as possible, because, who knows who or what you could offend.

But they went too far. I get it, some subjects are sensitive and better not allow posts about it, or if you do, make sure the comments are limited or even forbidden, but if you start by cutting people off from the truth because you prefer not to hear it, that is another matter. I guess everybody by know has come across the famous "Facebook police" and how ridiculous it sometimes is.

But what it especially created, it seems, is a whole culture of people who get offended by anything. and that just isn´t right. I was brought up with the idea that there was freedom of speech and yes, even i know that sometimes it is better to just shut up, ignore someone, or just block someone out of your life, and i don´t mean just online, but if someone called you a name, we learned to deal with it. If you saw something happening that you didn´t agree with, there were two choices, either you came in between or just shut up because our parents told us, everybody can use words, its actions that count.

And like that we grew up, we became adults, we learned that no, not everything is always going to go our way and when it doesn´t, deal with it. You can have problems but there are many solutions, don´t cry about everything and you know, try to do your best in life and try to be the best version of yourself. And you know what? We got through it, some better than others but most people i know, despite sometimes very bad moments in their lives, have a pretty happy life.

But that is what happened with social media, suddenly we needed a moral compass that not only would apply to our close surroundings but would be neutral enough for the whole world, and that just isn´t right. People are people, with their similarities but also with sometimes huge differences, and that is good, because otherwise we are heading for a civilization that is going to be very, very boring.

But it wasn´t only that of course, it seems that nowadays everything that makes you unique gets decided for you. What you should eat or drink, what is the correct way of living or not and what gets me the most is, they try to dictate you how you should feel about something and going from that norm sometimes can be a big no no. And why i hear you ask? Because sometimes an idea, a thought, becomes a movement, and sometimes that movement becomes so big because of big business being behind it, that it is even considered wrong to ask the question, wait a minute, can i check if this is even true?

A prime example of this is climate change.

The whole issue of climate change is a prime example of how social media is trying to influence our minds and our lives.

When you look at it, it really started about 20 years ago, in the beginning of the 2000s. At first they called it global warming but that they had to change very quickly because it simply turned out that that was a false statement.

So instead they called it climate change, a title that says everything and nothing at the same time.

But who were "they"?

Well that is very simple really. It all started with the automobile industry and not the way you think. Where it comes down to is the fact that back in the 90s new car sales were going down and the reason for that was also very simple, they were making cars too good.

In the past, if you were a daily driver, your car would last you about 4 or 5 years. Yes of course you could keep it longer time but then it would be at a cost, parts that need to be replaced etc...

But from the 90s on more and more brands came on the market and what did the big established brands do? They went the way of quality. And for sure, that is not a bad thing, the problem is, if you make something too good, people won´t feel the need buy a new one so often.

Electric cars, hybrids, was something that had been in the pipeline already for many, many years. The problem was, people didn´t see the need for it. But the industry itself had already invested millions in to these new technologies, if not billions. Because let´s get one thing straight, the automobile industry is not run by idiots, even they could predict that there would be an evolution in more ecological responsible vehicle, simply because the natural resources won´t last us forever.

But what could they do to get people involved, more interested in these new technologies?

Enter, the politicians. The big car companies started to lobby politicians because they were the link to the people. But also, politicians also have the power to promote or to shut down scientifical programs. So one would serve the other. Politicians asked scientists to come up with studies that would show how bad we are for the planet, scientists in turn would get more approval for projects, more funding and once the public would start to warm to the idea of a climate change, they would start to live more eco-friendly and buy electric or hybrid cars and like that make the automobile industry very happy.

And of course social media was the perfect tool for all of this also.

And guess what happened, the people bought and ate it like it were fresh baked cookies. Because if scientists are saying it, it must be true, right?

Well, the fact is, no, double no.

Yes there is a problem of pollution, nobody is going to deny that. But do we really have that much of an impact on climate change? If you look at the long history of our planet you will see that it isn't so.

Of course it is easy for scientists to come up with all kinds of graphics to show that we are now in an accelerated climate change, but that is only of you don´t look at the more larger picture.

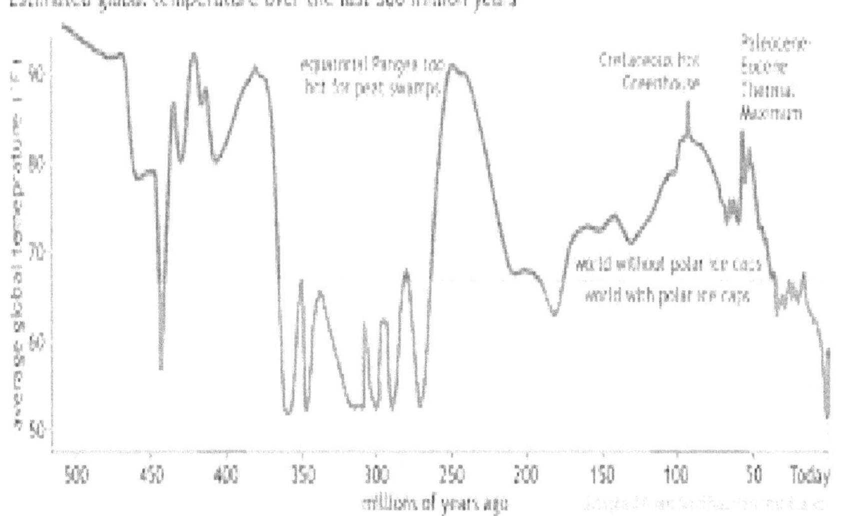

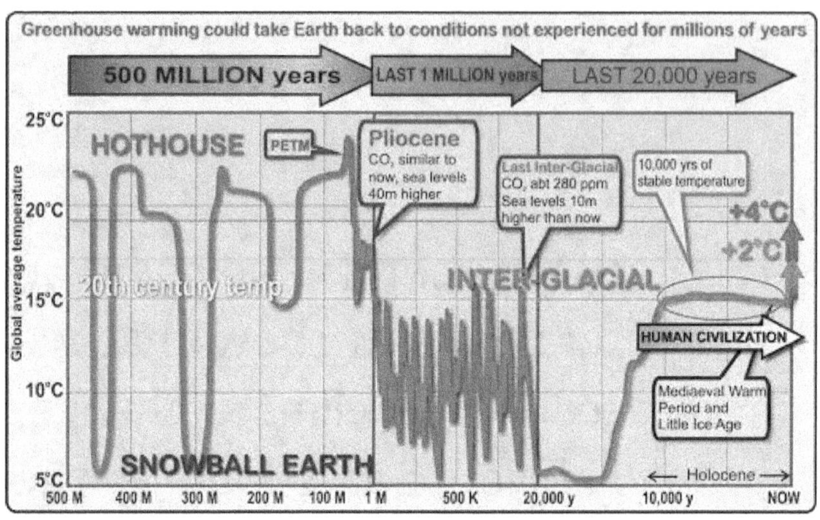

If you look at it more closer you will see that nothing special is going on really, in fact it is very average what is happening now. Also, take in mind that we are still recovering from the last mini ice-age in the middle ages.

But the truth is, we are far from having an abnormal climate change, in fact, we are long overdue. That this happens now, in an age were people are getting better informed, or supposed to be, does not change the fact.

But they got what they wanted and it is even more frightening that of all people most of us are now listening to the advice of a teenager instead of just using our own brain capacity.

Greta Thunberg has started a whole movement that spread around the globe.

Without any formal education in the matter but fueled by social media, she managed to get even more people convinced that, yes, we are the big factor in this whole climate change debate. Meanwhile the automobile industry are laughing their asses off.

But as if this wasn´t enough, we didn´t see nothing yet because 2020 would have something in store for us that would take everyone by surprise and show and explain that we really haven´t learned nothing of the past.

8.THE VIRUS

It was the beginning of 2020 and suddenly news was coming from China, Wuhan to be exact, about a new virus that was among the population and that we should be aware.

I am sure everyone of you, just like me, didn´t lose a minute of sleep about this. It was far away, it was not the first time strange things happens in China etc....

But then, it started to spread to out, cases began to pop up in Europe, people started to die and before we really knew what was going on, it had spread all over the world. And with this, not only were governments all over the globe forced to take action but also, the first conspiracy theories began to pop up.

The western world was forced to go in a lockdown and most countries did just that. At this first you could hear voices stating that this was a biological attack of China on the rest of the world. Soon followed by Russia being involved, just because of their ties to communism and the fact that there didn´t seem to be a lot of victims in Russia.

But this was just the beginning of a story that, in large part thanks to social media, became so much bigger than it actually should have been.

But let´s go back first, just a little bit, to the year 2009, when we had the Mexican flue.

It actually started more or less the same way, a new variety of the flue was among the people and steps were taken to get it under control. although this new kind of flue was not nearly as deadly as COVID-19, people did die, measurements were taken all over the world and you know what, people were ok with that. The one differential in all of this was social media. We had to follow certain rules, and believe me, i know, i got married that year, in Mexico, and there were regulations for guests entering and leaving Mexico, guests at my wedding that returned to Europe were forced to take tests or just had to go in to quarantine and when i myself went to Europe just a couple weeks later, the same thing happened to me.

But no worries, it was something that we had to careful about, we just had to follow the rules and everything would be ok. And i must say, and this is just personally, we didn´t think too much about it. My friends in Europe even joked about it, asking me if it was safe for them to see me. We laughed about it, drank a beer together and pretty soon, there was no more talk about the Mexican flue, everybody just had followed the rules and that was it.

But let´s get back to the corona virus.

It became clear pretty soon that something had to be done and so the governments, most of them, did just that. We went in to lockdown, trying to reduce the risk of infection.

But as soon as we went in to lockdown, social media exploded. It was all a big conspiracy. First they blamed the Chinese, stating that they released this virus as a biological weapon against the western world and like get control over the world economy.

But that didn´t seem logical at the same time. Why would the Chinese attack the western world when most of their money they were making these days came from the west?

So bye to that theory. Then came the next. The US government was working in secret in China and they released the virus in order to reclaim the economic throne in the world, a big reset as they called it.

Of course this didn´t hold up either. Why would the US need a virus while their biggest companies still were doing very well in the global economy? Another argument of this "big reset" theory was they were going to basically enslave the world population and create a world where we just can go to work and for the rest do as little as possible. Well anyone who can think logically for two seconds can tell you that this would only harm the big companies, they in fact depend on people having as much free time as possible, in order so they can spend money.

So what was next?

Enter Bill Gates again. He was and is an evil

genius master mind . Because didn´t he state that we have to kill off a large portion of the world population?

Well in fact, he didn´t. The only thing Gates ever said was that we have to do something about the over population. Implement a new way of thinking in a lot of countries where large families still is the norm. so we can take down this overgrowth of the human population.

But this wasn´t the only plan of Gates. Being the evil genius and with 5G lurking around the corner, he would make sure that everyone would be vaccinated and that within this vaccine there would be a micro chip and like that all the people would be controlled because they could follow your every movement.

Now, really? I mean really really? First of all, most of us are not interesting enough to be followed, let´s get that straight. And second, we have come so far in technology by now that if they want to track you or see what you are doing on your PC, tablet, smartphone etc..they don´t need a micro chip for that, they would find out in a heartbeat.

So let´s put Gates aside shall we? I mean, yes he is very rich and very influential but is he an evil genius, i guess not.

But let´s get back to virus itself. That also was an issue. Because why were we in a lockdown? Scientists from all over the world came out of the woodworks stating that this virus was nothing more than a bad flue, that the percentage of people dying wasn´t nearly high enough to panic and that there were very simple solutions.

And of course, through social media all these "experts" seemed to become the new messiahs. Anyone that took the virus seriously was branded a sheep because, couldn´t you people see what was going on?

Well yes, we saw what was going on and also, and more important, we took the time to check these claims that were floating around. And what came was very simple. Most of these "experts" were either former employees of big companies with still a chip on their shoulder, or they were just alternative medical researchers, making claims that couldn´t be held up by real research.

But no matter what you would tell these believers in order to convince them, it didn´t matter, this was al an evil masterplan, organized by the New World Order. Because that where we were at this point, suddenly the NWO was behind all of this.

The only problem is, as i explained before, where would the established World Order go?

There is well established military industrial complex that isn´t going anywhere. Sure, the filling in of the seats can sometimes change but it will always be same major players.

But no no, there was evidence of NWO, people were very fast to point out that there such things as the Bohemian Grove club and the Bilderberg group and that they planned this.

Now let´s have a closer look at these organizations.

The Bohemian Grove club is a club that meets every year in mid July. Very little is known about who attends and even less is known about the topics that are being discussed there.

The only thing we know for sure is that, yes, some very powerful people attend the BHC, but that is about it. What is being said or decided there, nobody knows and yes, it might even be that some decissions that are being made there can affect the world, but that would be more to keep the people who are already in power, even more secured.

So what about the Bilderberg group?

Well here there is less of a secret. It is an annual meeting of some very powerful and influential people from Europe and America mostly. They come together to discuss the state of the world in it´s whole and also discuss where our economies should work towards to.

But, a lot of those meetings are open to the public and we know exactly what is being discussed but even if some meeting are done in secret, we come back to the same point, namely that of the established World

Order.

And then of course, last but not least, the issue of Big Pharma.

It is simply ridiculous to think they are behind all of this. Sure, the were responsible for the virus getting out in the first place, i think nobody would argue about that fact, but they really benefit? Was this a plan to make them even richer? The simple answer, again, is no.

In fact, the pharmaceutical industry isn´t too pleased with this virus. first of all there is the damage to their image in general, because the trust of the people in them has gone down. But do they stand to get even richer? No, not even that. Sure, the vaccines by the different companies will mean a big paycheck but they lost money in other areas. The population in general has become more cautious, started to live cleaner and healthier, which in turn means less people getting sick and less income for the industry. Also, because of this virus almost everything that was in development was put on hold in order to get the vaccine, so less new drugs coming out and again less income.

So, in short, Big pharma isn´t behind it neither.

And like that we come to a close.

No there isn´t a New World Order that is going to take over the world, no Bill Gates is not an evil master mind etc...

We just had a relatively long time where everything more or less stayed status quo, apart from the technological advances we made. But anyone with a bit of a logical mind could have predicted that we were already long overdue for a major catastrophe.

And just like before, we will come thru this, most of us will survive and before we know it, this will all be a bad memory.

So stay safe, follow the rules, how hard it might be sometimes and be happy.

www.ingramcontent.com/pod-product-compliance
Lightning Source LLC
Chambersburg PA
CBHW051248150726
48001CB00019B/1710